Introduction to

Metadata
Pathways to Digital Information

Edited by Murtha Baca

Getty Information Institute

Cover image: Detail of *The Meeting of the Three Kings, with David and Isaiah*, before 1480, by the Master of the Saint Bartholomew Altarpiece, from the collection of the J. Paul Getty Museum, Los Angeles, California. Oil and gold leaf on panel, 24³/₄ × 28¹/₈ in. (62.8 × 71.2 cm.).

Library of Congress Cataloging-in-
Publication Data
Introduction to metadata : pathways
   to digital information / edited by
   Murtha Baca.
      p.   cm.
   ISBN 0-89236-533-1
      1. Database management.
2. Metadata. 3. World Wide Web
(Information retrieval system)
I. Baca, Murtha. II. Getty Informa-
tion Institute.
QA76.9.D3I599 1998
005.7—dc21   98-35383
                          CIP

Acknowledgments

This publication is dedicated to all those who preached the gospel of data standards long before the word "metadata" became fashionable—first and foremost among them Eleanor Fink, who realized more than a decade ago that the only way to make information accessible in the networked environment was to establish descriptive standards through careful consensus-building.

Thanks also go to those who have spent long hours analyzing, comparing, and mapping metadata standards: Joseph Busch, former Program Manager for Standards and Research Databases, Getty Information Institute; Patricia Harpring, Senior Editor of the Vocabulary Program, Getty Information Institute; and Ricky Erway, Program Officer of Integrated Information Services, The Research Libraries Group.

We are grateful to research assistant Christina Yamanaka and especially to editor Nancy Bryan.

Contents

Foreword

Thanks to the rapid evolution of the World Wide Web, universal access to digitized images and art information—no matter where they reside—appears to be at our fingertips. But if we envision this new digital frontier as a library, with indexing guidelines providing descriptions, finding aids, and references to related materials, we will be disappointed. Lack of shared standards and inconsistencies in recording and indexing digital information—not technology—are obstacles to easy and seamless use of future global digital libraries.

The Getty Information Institute has long been aware of the need to agree upon standards to enable users to access and retrieve cultural heritage information on networks. Together with the College Art Association, the Information Institute took the lead in forming the Art Information Task Force. The three-year dialogue between art historians and information providers led to agreement on the descriptive information needed to share and exchange art information for research purposes. This initiative produced *Categories for the Description of Works of Art*, which define common ground for agreement on items of information that should be included in automated descriptions of works of art.

The Information Institute is also spearheading a complementary initiative, called Protecting Cultural Objects in the Global Information Society, that has reached wide consensus on the core data needed to uniquely identify cultural objects. To help stem the tide of illicit trade, participants in this initiative devised "Object ID," a checklist that will help those who protect cultural objects to rapidly communicate descriptions of art works to aid in their recovery.

While standards such as *Categories for the Description of Works of Art* and Object ID represent the "skeleton" for structuring art information in disparate systems and places, Web metadata is the skin or membrane that can be grafted onto digital resources to make them accessible in meaningful ways.

We are on the brink of what is still only a fledgling global information society. The goal of this publication is to help the communities that we serve understand the road ahead if we are to create order and harmony out of the current chaotic state of the World Wide Web, and truly begin to create "virtual databases" and digital libraries of high-quality cultural heritage information.

Eleanor Fink
Director
Getty Information Institute

Introduction

This publication is intended as a primer for an important but misunderstood—and still evolving—aspect of the age of information: metadata.*

Professionals who are deeply involved in the development and implementation of information standards have contributed to this publication: Anne Gilliland-Swetland presents an overview, outlining types, functions, attributes, and characteristics of metadata, with examples from the "real world." Her essay seeks to dispel common myths, and to demonstrate the importance and role of metadata in the current information universe. Tony Gill's essay focuses on metadata in the context of the World Wide Web, and examines three important emerging Web metadata standards. Willy Cromwell-Kessler discusses the importance of mapping different metadata standards to facilitate interoperability, and identifies some of the concomitant issues, benefits, and necessary future steps.

We also include a a chart that maps nine metadata standards for cultural heritage information and Web resource discovery. A glossary and list of acronyms and Web addresses complete this "guidebook" for travelers through the world of digital information.

Metadata, particularly for the World Wide Web, is still in its infancy, and will surely continue to evolve. We believe that this issue is so important as to warrant a publication at this relatively early stage, to enable those with a stake in the debate (everyone from librarians to museum professionals to those who intend to make information available on a network) to avoid mistakes and wasted effort, and to make informed decisions about the information they seek to record and disseminate.

---

* The authors of this publication are well aware that the noun "metadata" is plural, and should therefore take plural verbs. We have opted to treat it as a singular noun, to avoid awkward locutions.

Defining Metadata

Anne J. Gilliland-Swetland
Department of Library and Information Science,
University of California, Los Angeles

Metadata, literally "data about data," has become a ubiquitous term that is
understood in different ways by many different professional communities.
As these communities, and also repositories and computer systems, come
together to make the information age a reality, it is essential that we
understand the critical roles that different types of metadata can play in
the development of effective, authoritative, flexible, scalable, and robust
cultural heritage and information systems.

Traditionally, cultural heritage and information professionals
such as museum registrars, library cataloguers, and archivists have used the
term *metadata* to refer to cataloging or indexing information that they create to arrange, describe, and otherwise enhance access to an information
object. Since the 1960s, libraries, aided by internationally recognized
cataloging rules and structural and content standards such as MARC
(MAchine-Readable Cataloging format) and specialized subject headings
such as LCSH (*Library of Congress Subject Headings*), have shared
descriptive metadata using automated systems such as online public
access catalogs. Descriptive theory and practices vary considerably owing
to the differing professional and cultural missions of museums, archives,
and libraries, however, and many additional standards are now emerging
that attempt to reconcile the commonalities and exploit the differences
between these communities. Indeed, not since the latter part of the nine-
teenth century has there been such an exciting—but also potentially
bewildering—array of organizational and descriptive schema from which
information professionals can choose.

But there is more to metadata than description; a more inclusive
conceptualization of metadata is needed as information professionals
consider the range of their activities that may end up being incorporated
into digital information systems. Repositories also create metadata relating
to the administration, accessioning, preservation, and use of collections.
Acquisition records, exhibition catalogs, and use data are all examples of
these, even though they are largely still created in paper form. Today,

integrated information systems such as virtual museums and digital libraries and archives include digital versions of actual collection content as well as descriptions of that content. Incorporating other types of metadata into such systems reaffirms their importance in administering collections and maintaining their integrity. Paul Conway alludes to this fact when he discusses the impact of digitization on preservation:

> The digital world transforms traditional preservation concepts from protecting the physical integrity of the object to specifying the creation and maintenance of the object whose intellectual integrity is its primary characteristic.[1]

In an environment where a user can gain unmediated access to content over a network, metadata is required to indicate the name and nature of the repository, to certify the authenticity and context of the content, and to provide some of the data an information professional might have provided in a physical reference or research setting. Moreover, thoughtfully constructed metadata may also provide additional access points to content that might be exploited by digital information systems.

In less traditional information domains, the term *metadata* acquires an even broader scope. An Internet resource provider might use metadata to refer to information being encoded into HTML metatags for the purposes of making a Web site easier to find. Individuals digitizing images might think of metadata as the information they enter into the header field for the digital file to record information about the image, the imaging process, and image rights. A social science data archivist might use the term to refer to the systems and research documentation necessary to run and interpret a magnetic tape containing raw research data. An electronic records archivist might use the term to refer to all the contextual, processing, and use information needed to identify and document the scope, authenticity, and integrity of a record in an electronic system. In all of these diverse interpretations, metadata not only identifies and describes an information object; it also documents how that object behaves, its function and use, its relationship to other information objects, and how it should be managed.

All of these perspectives on metadata become important in the development of networked digital information systems, but they lead to a very broad conception of metadata. To understand this conception better, it is helpful to break it down into distinct categories—administrative, descriptive, preservation, use, and technical metadata—that reflect key aspects of metadata functionality. Table 1 defines each of these metadata

---

[1] Paul Conway, *Preservation in the Digital World*, Washington, DC: Commission on Preservation and Access, 1996. http://clir.stanford.edu/cpa/reports/conway2/.

Table 1 **Different Types of Metadata and Their Functions**

Type	Definition	Examples
Administrative	Metadata used in managing and administering information resources	• Acquisition information • Rights and reproduction tracking • Documentation of legal access requirements • Location information • Selection criteria for digitization • Version control
Descriptive	Metadata used to describe or identify information resources	• Cataloging records • Finding aids • Specialized indexes • Hyperlinked relationships between resources • Annotations by users
Preservation	Metadata related to the preservation management of information resources	• Documentation of physical condition of resources • Documentation of actions taken to preserve physical and digital versions of resources, e.g., data refreshing and migration
Technical	Metadata related to how a system functions or metadata behaves	• Hardware and software documentation • Digitization information, e.g., formats, compression ratios, scaling routines • Tracking of system response times • Authentication and security data, e.g., encryption keys, passwords
Use	Metadata related to the level and type of use of information resources	• Exhibition records • Use and user tracking • Content re-use and multi-versioning information

categories and gives examples of common functions that each might perform in a digital information system.

In addition to there being different types of metadata and metadata functions, metadata also exhibits many different characteristics. Table 2 indicates some of the key attributes of metadata, with examples.

Metadata creation and management have become a very complex mix of manual and automatic processes and layers created by many different functions and individuals at different points in the life of an information object.[2] Figure 1 illustrates the different phases through which information objects typically move during their life in a digital environment.[3] As they move through each phase, the objects acquire layers of metadata that can be associated with the objects in several ways. Metadata can be contained within the same envelope as the information object, for example, in the form of header information for an image file.

---

[2] An information object is a digital item or group of items, regardless of type or format, that can be addressed or manipulated as a single object by a computer. This concept can be confusing in that it can be used to refer both to actual content (such as digitized images) and to content surrogates (such as catalog records or finding aids).

[3] Modified from the Information Life Cycle, *Social Aspects of Digital Libraries: A Report of the UCLA–NSF Social Aspects of Digital Libraries Workshop*, Los Angeles, CA: Graduate School of Education and Information Studies, November 1996: 7.

Table 2   **Attributes and Characteristics of Metadata**

Attribute	Characteristics	Examples
Source of metadata	Internal metadata generated by the creating agent for an information object at the time when it is first created or digitized	• File names and header information • Directory structures • File format and compression scheme
	External metadata relating to an information object that is created later, often by someone other than the original creator	• Registrarial and cataloging records • Rights and other legal information
Method of metadata creation	Automatic metadata generated by a computer	• Keyword indexes • User transaction logs
	Manual metadata created by people	• Descriptive surrogates such as catalog records and Dublin Core metadata
Nature of metadata	Lay metadata created by persons who are neither subject nor information specialists, often the original creator of the information object	• Metatags created for a personal Web page • Personal filing systems
	Expert metadata created by either subject or information specialists, often not the original creator of the information object	• Specialized subject headings • MARC records • Archival finding aids
Status	Static metadata that never changes once it has been created	• Title, provenance, and date of creation of an information resource
	Dynamic metadata that may change with use or manipulation of an information object	• Directory structure • User transaction logs • Image resolution
	Long-term metadata necessary to ensure that the information object continues to be accessible and usable	• Technical format and processing information • Rights information
	Short-term metadata, mainly of a transactional nature	• Preservation management documentation
Structure	Structured metadata that conforms to a predictable standardized or unstandardized structure	• MARC • TEI and EAD • local database formats
	Unstructured metadata that does not conform to a predictable structure	• Unstructured note fields and annotations
Semantics	Controlled metadata that conforms to a standardized vocabulary or authority form	• AAT • ULAN • AACR2
	Uncontrolled metadata that does not conform to any standardized vocabulary or authority form	• Free-text notes • HTML metatags
Level	Collection metadata relating to collections of information objects	• Collection-level record, e.g., MARC record or finding aid • Specialized index
	Item metadata relating to individual information objects, often contained within collections	• Transcribed image captions and dates • Format information

Metadata can be attached to the information object through bidirectional pointers or hyperlinks. Relationships between metadata and information objects, and between different aspects of metadata, can also be documented by registering them with a metadata registry.[4] As systems designers

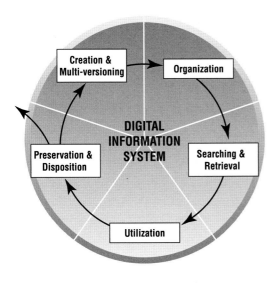

Creation and multi-versioning: Objects enter a digital information system by being created digitally or by being converted into digital format. Multiple versions of the same object may be created for preservation, research, dissemination, or even product development purposes. Some administrative and descriptive metadata may be included by the creator.

Organization: Objects are automatically or manually organized into the structure of the digital information system, and additional metadata for those objects may be created through registration, cataloging, and indexing processes.

Searching and retrieval: Stored and distributed objects are subject to search and retrieval by users. The computer system creates metadata that tracks retrieval algorithms, user transactions, and system effectiveness in storage and retrieval.

Utilization: Retrieved objects are utilized, reproduced, and modified. Metadata related to user annotations, rights tracking, and version control may be created.

Preservation and disposition: Information objects undergo processes such as refreshing, migration, and integrity checking to ensure their continued availability. Information objects that are inactive or no longer necessary may be discarded. Metadata may document both preservation and disposition activities.

Figure 1 **The life cycle of objects contained in a digital information system**

increasingly respond to the need to incorporate and manage metadata in information systems, many additional mechanisms for associating metadata with information objects are likely to become available.

Dispelling Some Common Myths about Metadata

1. *Metadata does not have to be digital.* Cultural heritage professionals have been creating metadata for as long as they have been managing collections. Increasingly, such metadata will be incorporated into digital information systems.
2. *Metadata relates to more than the description of an object.* While many museum, archives, and library professionals are most familiar with the term in association with description or cataloging, metadata can also indicate the context, management, processing, preservation, and use of the resources being described.

---

[4] Joint Workshop on Metadata Registries, Workshop Report, Draft 1.6, 1997. http://www.lbl.gov/~olken/EPA/Workshop/report.html.

3. *Metadata can come from a variety of sources.* It can be supplied by a human (a creator, information professional, or user), created automatically by a computer, or inferred through a relationship to another resource, such as a hyperlink.

4. *Metadata continues to accrue during the life of an information object or system.* Metadata is created, modified, and sometimes even disposed of at many points during the life of a resource.

Why Is Metadata Important?

As illustrated by the preceding discussion, metadata is a complex construct that can be expensive to create and maintain. How then can one justify the costs and efforts involved? The development of the World Wide Web and other networked digital information systems has provided information professionals with many opportunities, while at the same time requiring them to confront issues that they have not had occasion to explore before. Judiciously crafted metadata, wherever possible conforming to national and international standards, has become the tool that information professionals are using to exploit some of these opportunities, as well as to address some of the new issues:

Increased accessibility: Effectiveness of searching can be significantly enhanced through the existence of rich, consistent metadata. Metadata can also make it possible to search across multiple collections or to create virtual collections from materials that are distributed across several repositories, but only if the descriptive metadata is the same or can be mapped across each site. Digital information systems and emerging metadata standards developed by different professional communities but incorporating some common data elements such as Encoded Archival Description (EAD), the Text Encoding Initiative (TEI), and the Dublin Core are making it easier for a user to negotiate between descriptive surrogates of information objects and digital versions of the objects themselves, and to search at both the item and collection level within and across information systems.

Retention of context: Museum, archival, and library repositories do not simply hold objects. They maintain collections of objects that have complex interrelationships among each other and associations with people, places, movements, and events. In the digital world it is not difficult for a single object from a collection to be digitized and then to become separated from both its own cataloging information and its relationship to the other objects in the same collection. Metadata plays a critical role in documenting and maintaining those relationships, as well as in indicating the authenticity, structural integrity, and comprehensiveness of information objects. For example, when documenting the content, context, and structure of an archival record what helps to distinguish that record from decontextualized information is metadata in the form of an archival finding aid.

Expanding use: Digital information systems for museum and archives collections make it easier to disseminate digital versions of unique objects to users around the globe who, for reasons of geography, economics, or other barriers, might otherwise never have had an opportunity to view them. With new communities of users, however, come new challenges of how to make the materials most intellectually accessible to them. These new communities of users may have needs that differ significantly from those of the traditional users around whom many existing information services have been designed. For example, teachers and school children may want to search for and use information objects quite differently than scholarly researchers do. Metadata can document changing uses of systems and content, and that information can in turn feed back into systems development decisions. Well-structured metadata can also facilitate an almost infinite number of ways to search for information, present results, and even manipulate information objects without compromising their integrity.

Multi-versioning: The existence of information and cultural objects in digital form has heightened interest in the ability to create multiple and variant versions of those objects. This process may be as simple as creating both a high-resolution copy for preservation or scholarly research purposes and a low-resolution thumbnail image that can be rapidly transferred over a network for quick reference purposes. Or, it may entail creating variant or derivative forms to be used, for example, in publications, exhibitions, or schoolrooms. In either case, there must be metadata that links the multiple versions and captures what is the same and what is different about each version. The metadata must also be able to distinguish what is qualitatively different between digitized versions and the hard copy original or parent object.

Legal issues: Metadata allows repositories to track the many layers of rights and reproduction information that exist for information objects and their multiple versions. Metadata also documents other legal or donor requirements that have been imposed on objects—for example, privacy concerns or proprietary interests.

Preservation: If digital information objects that are currently being created are to have a chance of surviving migrations through successive generations of computer hardware and software, or removal to entirely new delivery systems, they will need to have metadata that enables them to exist independently of the system that is currently being used to store and retrieve them. Technical, descriptive, and preservation metadata that documents how a digital information object was created and maintained, how it behaves, and how it relates to other information objects will all be essential. It should be noted that for the information objects to remain accessible and intelligible over time, it will also be essential to preserve and migrate this metadata.

System improvement and economics: Benchmark technical data, much of which can be collected automatically by a computer, is necessary to evaluate and refine systems in order to make them more effective and efficient from a technical and economic standpoint. The data can also be used in planning for new systems.

Conclusion

If thorough and consistent metadata has been created, it is possible to conceive of its use in an almost infinite number of new ways to meet the needs of nontraditional users, for multi-versioning, and for data mining. The resources and intellectual and technical design issues that metadata development and management entail are not trivial, however. For example, some key questions that information professionals must resolve as they develop digital information systems and objects include deciding which aspects of metadata are essential to what they wish to achieve, and how detailed they need each type of metadata to be: in other words, how much is enough and how much is too much. There will probably always be important trade-offs between the costs of developing and managing metadata to meet current needs and creating enough metadata that can be capitalized upon for future, often unanticipated, reasons.

What we do know is that many types of metadata will prove critical to the continued physical and intellectual accessibility and utility of digital information resources and the information objects that they contain. In this sense, metadata provides us with the Rosetta Stone that will enable us to decode information objects and to transform them into knowledge in the cultural heritage and information systems of the twenty-first century.

Metadata and the World Wide Web

Tony Gill
Art, Design, Architecture and Media Information Gateway
and Visual Arts Data Service, Surrey Institute of Art and Design

Introduction

"Metadata" is not a user-friendly term. However, the underlying concept, at least in the context of this essay, is relatively straightforward; metadata is simply meaningful data describing another discrete data object (notwithstanding the more philosophical problem of defining what, exactly, constitutes a data object).

This means that the relationship between a data object and the metadata describing it is functionally identical to the relationship between a book and its library catalog record, for example, or a museum's object and its corresponding record in a collections management system. In the context of this essay, then, metadata is a structured description of a data object.

Catalogs made up of structured object descriptions can be found wherever there are large collections of objects that need to be managed. The computerized inventory used by a warehouse to control stock levels contains fundamentally the same type of information as a museum's collections management database, a library's bibliographic database, or a domestic card index of an individual's compact disc collection; each individual descriptive record is an attempt to capture in a concise and manageable form the key defining features, or the essence, of the object it describes.

Ideally, the structure of the descriptive records in a given database is designed to enable the information to be searched, sorted, and displayed in ways that make it easier to effectively use and manage the collection that is being described. Exactly what this structure should be will be determined by the collections management tasks that need to be carried out, the degree of homogeneity of the objects in the collection, and the database designer's skill in capturing and structuring the essence of the objects.

The Rise and Rise of the World Wide Web

People, in general, do not have limitless memory capabilities, and so the importance of descriptive catalogs for accessing and managing collections increases in proportion to the size of the collection being described. The lack of such a catalog is one of the most serious drawbacks of the World Wide Web, the vast network of hypermedia pages that without doubt constitutes the world's largest and fastest-growing collection of data objects.

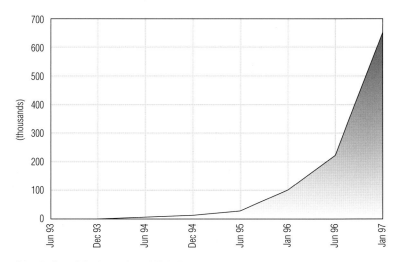

Figure 2   **Growth in the number of Web sites**

Accurate current statistics about the growth of the Web are hard to come by, but even the most conservative estimates indicate a frightening rate of growth; Matthew Gray's Web Growth Summary[5] suggests that the number of Web sites on the Internet grew from just 130 in June 1993 to an estimated 650,000 in January 1997, an increase of 500,000 percent in 42 months, and this estimate is based on the extremely conservative definition that a Web site is a collection of documents that have URLs (Uniform Resource Locators) beginning with a unique hostname:

> That is, http://www.mit.edu/people/mkgray/ and http://www.mit.edu/madlibs are part of the same site, but a document http://Web.mit.edu/ is a separate site.[6]

Although it is essential to make this kind of simplistic distinction in order to obtain any meaningful statistical data, it also means that the

---

[5] Data from Matthew Gray, Massachusetts Institute of Technology (http://www.mit.edu/people/mkgray/net/).

[6] Ibid.

figure of 650,000 is a gross underestimation of the true growth of the Web; Internet Service Providers, for example, may provide hundreds or even thousands of customers with Web space on a single Web host, each of which would have the same unique hostname, but would nonetheless be considered by most people to be unique individual Web sites.

Finding Needles in a Global Haystack

Unfortunately, neither the Internet nor the World Wide Web was originally designed with the cataloging of their contents in mind; the TCP/IP suite of network protocols that enables the basic infrastructure of the Internet to function is solely a transport layer, concerned with getting packets of data from one point to another as quickly and reliably as possible, whereas the HyperText Transfer Protocol (or HTTP) deals only with the delivery of hyperlinked World Wide Web information.

This means that the existing network protocols provide no dedicated support for locating specific information resources available on the network. This sorry state of affairs falls very short of the vision of the Memex, a democratic global knowledge base originally proposed in 1945 by Vannevar Bush. The hypertext community's disappointment with the World Wide Web is clearly illustrated by this quote from Ted Nelson (the man who first coined the term "hypertext" in 1965), delivered at the Hypertext 97 conference:

> The reaction of the hypertext research community to the World Web is like finding out that you have a fully grown child. And it's a delinquent.[7]

Unsurprisingly, tools designed to address the resource location problem and help make sense of the Internet's vast array of information resources started to appear soon after the launch of the first Web browsers in the early 1990s; for example, Tim Berners-Lee founded the WWW Virtual Library shortly after inventing the Web itself, and Yahoo!, Lycos, and Webcrawler were all launched during 1994.

The tools currently available to help users find Web resources are many times larger and more powerful than their 1994 predecessors—they have to be, in order to keep up with the explosive growth in both the amount of information available and the number of users accessing it. However, there are still only two principal classes of Web resource-locating tools: directories and search engines.

---

[7] Ted Nelson, speaking at Hypertext 97, the Eighth ACM Conference on Hypertext, Southampton April 6–11, 1997. Source: Nick Gibbin's Trip Report on UK Web Focus Conference Centre at http://www.ukoln.ac.uk:8002/conference/.

Directories are lists of network resources created by real people, who select, catalog, and classify Web resources that they feel are suitable for their constituency. Directories can either be general, such as the World Wide Web Virtual Library[8] and Yahoo![9], or they can specialize in particular subject areas, such as the Art, Design, Architecture & Media Information Gateway (ADAM)[10] and the Edinburgh Engineering Virtual Library (EEVL).[11] Directories typically provide access to their links both by searching and by browsing a hierarchical set of subject headings.

Search engines, often called "spiders," "crawlers," or "robots," are automated systems that traverse the Web, visiting sites continuously, saving copies of the resources and their locations as they go in order to build up a huge catalog of fully indexed pages. They typically provide powerful searching facilities and extremely large result sets, which are "relevance-ranked" in an effort to make them usable.

However, there are serious problems with both the directory and search engine approaches; human-mediated directories provide good search precision at a broad subject level, and generally provide links to higher-quality information because of the human intervention in the indexing and classifying process, but this mediation is a labor-intensive and costly process that is not sufficiently scalable to provide comprehensive up-to-date coverage of the whole Web, much of which is highly transient.

Another problem with the hand-crafted approach to cataloging Web resources is deciding upon the level of detail of the resources to be described; should descriptions be created for Web sites as a whole, or should each page be cataloged individually? Clearly, a cost–benefit trade-off will always need to be made.

The search engines also suffer from a number of serious problems, which affect both their ability to provide a comprehensive current index and the likelihood that users will find what they are looking for even if it has been indexed:

- The Web crawling components are fully automated, which means that the Web resources are selected by software rather than by people, and are therefore variable in quality.
- Searching very large automatically indexed databases often results in extremely large result sets, which are frequently unusable despite increasingly sophisticated information retrieval tools, relevance ranking procedures, and context-aware artificial intelligence algorithms.

---

[8] WWW Virtual Library: http://vlib.stanford.edu/Overview.html

[9] Yahoo!: http://www.yahoo.com/

[10] ADAM: http://adam.ac.uk/

[11] EEVL: http://www.eevl.ac.uk/

- Increasingly, information on the Web is being generated "on the fly" from back-end databases (sometimes referred to as "the hidden Web"), which are beyond the indexing reach of the Web crawlers.
- As the volume of information on the Web increases, the amount of network bandwidth (information-carrying capacity) the crawlers will require in order to maintain reasonably current and comprehensive indices will eventually reach unacceptable levels; ethical "codes of conduct" for Web crawlers have already existed for some years.

Cataloging the Web

Although initially both directories and search engines seem to suffer from different types of problems, closer analysis shows that most, if not all, of the difficulties are the result of ambitions that are likely to prove untenable in the long term; the Web is simply getting too big for any single organization or service to catalog, irrespective of whether they use people or computers to generate their indices.

If there is a solution to the problem of resource discovery on the Web, it has to be based on some kind of distributed catalog (ironically, the WWW Virtual Library uses just such a distributed model; however, the altruistic efforts of its volunteer curators have proved insufficient to keep pace with the growth of the Web).

The necessary technical protocols for creating distributed resource discovery systems, such as Z39.50 and WHOIS++, are already available—interoperability at a technical level is no longer a problem. What is urgently needed now are the more abstract standards for information structure and content that will allow interoperability on the semantic level. However, in order to determine the most effective structure and content for Web metadata, the tasks that it will be required to perform need to be established.

The most common application of Web metadata is generally known as "resource discovery," because the metadata is intended to assist Web users in finding the information they are looking for; the availability of consistent, accurate, well-structured descriptions of Web resources would enable much greater search precision and more accurate relevance ranking of the large result sets typically retrieved by search engines, for example.

Metadata may also be used to provide short descriptions or evaluations of the resources located, which can help the user assess their suitability prior to downloading, or information about any access restrictions or rights implications that may prohibit the intended use of the information. Whether or not these applications are intrinsic parts of the resource discovery process, or are in fact separate applications of Web metadata, remains the subject of debate.

Metadata is also often used in the management and administration of digital networked resources; this type of "administrative metadata" is essential for ensuring that Web resources are kept up to date, for example, or are free of rights restrictions that may prohibit their distribution over the Internet.

Clearly, the information structure and content of any Web resource description record should capture the essence of the Web resources it describes, and facilitate the various tasks for which it was devised. Unfortunately, this is the point at which real-world complexities start to intrude; with such a large collection of objects to describe, spanning the breadth and depth of human knowledge and with tens of millions of users, the number of potential applications for Web metadata is limited only by the imagination. Consequently, consensus on the most appropriate structure and content for Web metadata remains elusive despite significant worldwide efforts; some of the more significant descriptive standards resulting from this metadata research are described below, and elsewhere in this guide.

One of the more interesting consequences of the metadata research taking place around the globe is that effective cataloging—historically perceived as an arcane art practiced only by librarians, museum curators, and archivists—is now becoming an issue for a much wider community. While there are undoubtedly many lessons that can and should be learned from the traditional custodians of information, there are also a number of new challenges unique to the pan-disciplinary, transglobal, multilingual, and multicultural networked environment of the Web that will require fresh approaches and new solutions.

Acceptance of the importance of controlled vocabularies and formal classification schemes for cataloging Web resources is becoming increasingly widespread, for example—a fact that most experienced cataloguers have taken for granted for decades (notwithstanding the fact that the sheer diversity of information on the Web highlights the shortcomings of the existing taxonomies for organizing the sum of human learning).

However, the sheer scale of the Web as an information space will require new applications of the old tools and skills, such as the use of thesauri by software programs to automatically expand users' queries to include synonyms or even translations of the query terms into alternate languages, or mappings between different classification schemes and terminology authorities. Similarly, the fact that a diverse range of vocabularies and classification schemes will need to coexist in the same information space means that computers must be able to identify the source authority for terms or class marks; consequently, scheme registries will be necessary in order to ensure that the labels used to identify the various authorities are unique and unambiguous.

Deciding upon the most appropriate level of detail for the resource descriptions is another issue that the would-be Web cataloguer must address: how much detail about a Web resource should a catalog record contain? How many catalog records should be created for a given Web resource? Increasing user expectations regarding retrieval capabilities, combined with the flexibility and diversity of the hypertext information environment, jointly conspire to render the analogy between cataloging Web resources and cataloging bibliographic resources only partially valid. No longer content with the traditional "author, title, keyword" searches offered by library catalogs, users now expect to be able to search for key-words within the subsection titles and actual body text of Web resources.

In an attempt to overcome these difficulties, the Art, Design, Architecture & Media Information Gateway is working with a software vendor to combine the directory and search engine approaches; trained subject librarians create high-quality site-level descriptions of carefully selected Web resources, which will then be augmented by full-text index-ing of the site using a Web crawler.

Another significant conceptual difficulty arises from the need to describe the relationships between networked resources and other objects: What exactly should metadata describe? Strictly speaking, metadata should describe the properties of an object that itself is data, for example a Web page, a digital image, or a database—which is analogous to the librarian's practice of cataloging "the thing in hand." For networked resources, how-ever, these properties are often not very interesting or useful for the pur-poses of discovery; for example, if researchers are interested in discovering images of famous artworks on the Web, they would generally search using the properties of the original artworks (e.g., CREATOR = Picasso, DATE = 1937), not the properties of the digital copies or "surrogates" of them (e.g., CREATOR = Scan-U-Like Imaging Labs Inc., DATE = 1998).

Both the "granularity" (level of detail) and "surrogacy" problems have at their root the need to describe the relationships among different objects (not all of which will exist on the Web) in the various records describing those objects; for example, a record describing a Web page within a site should indicate the site of which it is a part, and a scanned image of a Picasso painting on the Web should identify the painting from which it was derived.

Of course, none of the problems described above are new—the traditional guides to information resources, such as librarians, museum curators, and archivists, have been wrestling for decades with the seemingly impossible task of "modeling the world" in order to describe information resources. The urgent need to catalog the Web, however, has made these fundamentally epistemological issues significant for a new and much larger community.

Standards for Metadata on the Web

In order for metadata to be useful in the construction of a distributed catalog of the Web, it is essential that the structure and syntax of the information conform to widely supported standards, so that the semantics of the catalog records can be correctly interpreted across the various computers that make up the distributed catalog network.

A comprehensive overview of several current metadata standards is provided elsewhere in this guide. Here, I will discuss three current, closely related sets of metadata elements that are particularly pertinent for the Web environment: AltaVista <META> tags, the Dublin Core, and the Resource Description Framework.

AltaVista <META> Tags

The popular AltaVista search engine supports the use of two simple metadata elements, *Keywords* and *Description*, that can be embedded in Web resources using the HTML <META> tag. The *Keywords* information is used to assist relevance ranking, whereas information in the *Description* element is used in the results display to provide a more accurate summary of a Web resource.

Dublin Core

The Dublin Core Metadata Element Set (also known as "Dublin Core" or simply "DC") is a set of fifteen information elements that can be used to describe a wide variety of information resources on the Internet for the purpose of simple cross-disciplinary resource discovery. The fifteen elements are: *Contributor, Coverage, Creator, Date, Description, Format, Identifier, Language, Publisher, Relation, Rights, Source, Subject, Title,* and *Type.*

The elements and their meanings have been developed and refined by a group of librarians, information specialists, and subject specialists, through an ongoing consensus-building process that has to date included five international workshops and the active Meta2 mailing list.[12]

From the outset, the development of the Dublin Core element set has been influenced by a number of guiding philosophies:

---

[12] Archived at http://weeble.lut.ac.uk/lists/meta2/.

- The elements must be simple to understand and use, so that any creator of networked resources would be able to describe his/her own work without requiring extensive training.
- Every element is both optional and repeatable.
- The elements should be international and cross-disciplinary in scope and applicability.
- The element set should be extensible, to allow discipline- or task-specific enhancements.
- The most important strategic application of the element set would be for embedded descriptions of Web resources created by the resource authors, which means a syntax that could be accommodated within HTML's <META> tag.

Early adopters of the Dublin Core soon encountered the types of problems discussed in the previous section, which resulted in a number of additional refinements to the simple core element set:

- The *Warwick Framework*, a conceptual container architecture for diverse heterogeneous metadata packets; SGML and MIME implementations of the Warwick Framework have been developed, but perhaps the most important contribution is the formalization of requirements that led to the development of the Resource Description Framework.
- The *Canberra Qualifiers*, a set of three optional qualifiers (SUBELEMENT, SCHEME, and LANG) that can be used to refine the semantics of the element set to provide more precise information.
- An agreement that the only practical solution to the granularity and surrogacy issues described earlier is to use a separate metadata "set" or "packet" for each discrete object (item or collection, network resource or otherwise), and to describe the relationships between them using an enumerated list of relationship types.

However, the most significant outcome of the Dublin Core initiative is undoubtedly the international, cross-disciplinary consensus.

Resource Description Framework

The Resource Description Framework (RDF), produced as part of the World Wide Web Consortium's Metadata Activity, is a metadata application of XML, Extensible Markup Language, seen by most pundits as the successor to HTML and the future language of the Web. Its development was informed by previous work such as PICS (Platform for Internet Content Selection), the Dublin Core/Warwick Framework initiative, and the metadata activities of major software vendors such as Microsoft and Netscape.

The RDF will provide a flexible architecture for managing diverse, application-specific metadata packets that can be processed by machines. It will also allow the integration of digital signatures, which will enable organizations trusted by the public to "sign" metadata packets as honest and authentic descriptions of networked resources.

Metathreats and Metaopportunities

One of the main problems with the current HTML architecture for embedding metadata in Web resources is that it is open to abuse; as disreputable commercial organizations become increasingly aware of the financial benefits of appearing at the top of search engine results listings, efforts to fool the information retrieval algorithms, for example by repeating keywords in the metadata hundreds of times or using sexually explicit keywords in metadata, have increased markedly. Despite the best efforts of the search engines, this technique, known as "spamming," is creating a disincentive for Web authors wishing to embed descriptive metadata—rather than providing support for embedded metadata, the major search engines are having to employ an increasingly skeptical view of embedded metadata to foil the "spammers."

However, the Web is becoming increasingly secure, and the prospect of digital authentication will create opportunities for trusted information providers, such as libraries, museums, and government information services, to regain their role as the guardians of access to high-quality information resources on the World Wide Web of the twenty-first century.

Crosswalks, Metadata Mapping, and Interoperability: What Does It All Mean?

Willy Cromwell-Kessler
The Research Libraries Group

A major benefit of the emerging networked environment is the potential to integrate distinct but complementary information resources. These resources may range from the descriptive information in cataloging and citation databases to collections of whole-information resources such as digitized texts or images. They are frequently navigated by means of specifically structured, descriptive data—"metadata." Catalogs and citation databases themselves constitute specific types of metadata, while whole-information objects may be accompanied by such information. This type of metadata usually reflects the nature of the resource it describes as well as the goals and objects of the community it serves, and, consequently, may differ significantly from resource to resource. One mechanism for navigating between the various resources is the creation of "crosswalks" that result from analyzing and mapping the similarities of each metadata system. Creating maps from one metadata system to another is one of the most important mechanisms for reconciling their differences and enabling automated systems to interoperate in such a way that the goal of integrated access may be achieved.

Metadata systems differ in two overarching areas: content and structure. Content may differ in terms of the rules that govern its formulation and, since the electronic environment is increasingly international, in terms of language. The primary obstacle to integration, however, lies in the structure of different metadata systems, which may be composed of diverse data elements functioning at different levels, and designated in widely varying ways. Variant systems are often found even within a single subject community where competing metadata systems have developed in isolation—and where, before networked access, uniformity was deemed unnecessary.

In some cases it will be feasible for communities to come together to reconcile their metadata systems and develop community or cross-community standards, but such a solution, even when it is desirable, may be only hypothetical, since retrospective conversion of already existing or so-called "legacy" data is expensive and time-consuming. Where no single standard exists, integration will entail "translating" from one structured data system to another. In this view, a metadata crosswalk functions as a type of Rosetta Stone, providing the key to automating translation from one system to another. One common use of such mappings is illustrated by Z39.50 implementations, which require data conversion in order to allow the system a searcher uses to translate and retrieve data in a way that conforms to its own protocols.

As any linguist would tell us, translations between languages are rarely exact in a scientific sense. Similarly, since metadata systems differ in their breadth, depth, emphasis, and coverage, mapping between them is also often approximate. Among the issues that are most difficult to resolve are the following:

- Two or more concepts in one system may be represented by a single element in another system. This is not a problem when moving from the most inclusive to the less inclusive system, but reverse movement may be more difficult if not impossible.
- It may only be possible to map certain specifically delineated elements in one metadata system to general "notes" or "remarks" fields in another. Again, this makes reverse movement problematic.
- There may be no equivalence at all in one system for concepts expressed in others.
- There may be a cross-system tension between descriptive data intended for display and data intended to serve indexing and/or retrieval needs.

As these examples indicate, the process of mapping from one metadata system to another may entail difficult decisions about how to handle complex data issues. Since the goal of the mapping is to facilitate resource discovery and retrieval across a wide variety of sources, it is desirable that these decisions be made uniformly and, in most cases, not differ from one agency to another. Consequently, it becomes important to develop and maintain authoritative, comprehensive metadata registries that will offer definitions of the meaning, structure, and content designation of multiple metadata systems, and will include formal mappings of overlapping elements where appropriate.

True registries may be maintained by formal standards organizations such as the International Organization for Standardization (ISO), which has begun to address the issue of specification and standardization of data elements (see ISO 11179). However, until such comprehensive, formal registries of metadata elements can be developed, a number of agencies have started to develop and maintain less formal mappings that function as de facto registries. Examples of such informal sites are those maintained by the UK Office for Library and Information Networking (UKOLN) (http://ukoln.bath.ac.uk/metadata/interopability) and the Library of Congress (http://www.loc.gov/marc).

RLG/GII Metadata Crosswalk

The crosswalk included in this publication represents a preliminary version of a mapping that The Research Libraries Group is developing in collaboration with the Getty Information Institute. This mapping will be made available via the Web (at http://www.rlg.org), and will be updated and expanded at regular intervals; it will focus on cultural heritage information metadata systems. The metadata systems that are currently represented in this mapping cover a range of important element sets that emphasize description of works of art, museum objects, and other cultural heritage information, as well as some more general element sets:

- *Categories for the Description of Works of Art* (CDWA) offers an extensively articulated and very inclusive taxonomy of cultural heritage information. This standard, "the mother of cultural heritage metadata standards," provides detailed guidelines for scholarly description of art objects and their visual surrogates.
- The Object ID checklist defines the minimum information needed to track lost or stolen art objects, antiquities, and antiques.
- The CIMI Schema, derived from the CIDOC Data Model and *Categories for the Description of Works of Art*, is of central importance, since it defines a list of elements likely to exist in actual databases of cultural heritage information and has been used to inform the development of a Z39.50 profile for retrieval of such information.
- The FDA/ADAG (Foundation for Documents of Architecture/Architectural Drawings Advisory Group) *Guide to the Description of Architectural Drawings* categories provide guidelines for describing and accessing information on architectural documents.
- The MESL (Museum Educational Site Licensing project) categories, based on CDWA, were developed as part of a project exploring issues relating to higher education site licensing of museum images and related data.
- The VRA Core categories, which also took CDWA as their point of departure, are metadata for documenting works of art and

their visual surrogates. They are still a work in progress, having been developed by the Visual Resource Association's Data Standards Committee in an effort to delineate both the necessary elements and the correct approach for describing visual documents that represent cultural heritage and museum objects. The VISION (Visual Resources Sharing Information Online) project is a test of the application of the VRA core in a Web-based environment.

- REACH (Record Export for Art and Cultural Heritage) provides a common file format for the export of existing collections management records, intended to create a testbed of museum object records. This standard was designed to facilitate the extraction and "re-purposing" of existing museum management information as well as to stimulate discussion of issues surrounding the potential development of a community standard that would facilitate record sharing among museums.

- USMARC is included although it is not specifically devoted to cultural heritage information, since it is widely used and accepted in the United States and may be found in the cultural heritage repertoire. The MARC (MAchine-Readable Cataloging) format is a data structure for encoding records for books, archival materials, manuscripts, visual materials, etc. that has been entrenched in the library world for many years.

- The Dublin Core, which defines metadata elements for locating resources on the World Wide Web, is likewise more generally applicable. It is included here since there is great interest in exploring its role vis-à-vis cultural information on the Web.

A Crosswalk of Metadata Standards*

The chart on the following pages maps several important metadata standards to one another, showing where they intersect and how their coverage differs. Each of these standards can be said to represent a different "point of view"—while *Categories for the Description of Works of Art* provides broad, encompassing guidelines for the information elements needed to describe an art object from a scholarly or research point of view, Object ID codifies the minimum set of data elements (ten in all) needed to protect an object from theft and illicit traffic. The CIMI Schema defines data elements for "deep" museum information. The FDA guidelines focus on architectural documents, while MESL and the VRA Core Categories provide data elements for both the object and its visual surrogate. The goal of the REACH data elements is to provide a structure for exporting existing machine-readable data from heterogeneous museum collections management systems, and to analyze the research value of the resulting unified information. USMARC is a time-tested data standard used in the library world, while Dublin Core seeks to provide basic information elements or metadata categories to improve indexing and searching of World Wide Web resources.

Cultural heritage metadata standards not presented in this chart include SPECTRUM, a standard developed by the Museum Documentation Association (MDA) that defines twenty procedures carried out in museums, and their standard data requirements; the CIDOC Data Model, developed by the International Council of Museums Documentation Committee; the CIDOC Guidelines for Museum Object Standards; the International Council of Museums AFRICOM data standard; the AMICO (Art Museum Image Consortium) data dictionary; and the CHIN (Canadian Heritage Information Network) data dictionary, all of which map to *Categories for the Description of Works of Art*.

---

* Compiled by Murtha Baca, Joseph Busch, Willy Cromwell-Kessler, Tony Gill, and Patricia Harpring.

Metadata Standards Crosswalk

CDWA	Object ID	CIMI Schema	FDA	MESL
OBJECT/WORK (core)			Document Classification-Catalogue Level (core)	
			Document Classification-Group Type	
Object/Work-Type (core)	Type of Object	objectName	Document Classification-Document Type (core)	Object Type/Object Class/Object Name (required)
			Purpose-Purpose (Broad) (core)	Concepts/Functions
			Purpose-Purpose (Narrow)	
Object/Work-Components		quantity	Document Classification-Extent	Parts/Pieces
CLASSIFICATION (core)				
ORIENTATION/ARRANGEMENT				
TITLES OR NAMES (core)	Title	objectTitle bibliographicTitle	Group/Item Identification-Repository Title	Object Title/Caption (required)
			Group/Item Identification-Descriptive Title (core)	
			Group/Item Identification-Inscribed Title	
STATE				Edition/State
EDITION				Edition/State
MEASUREMENTS				
Measurements-Dimensions	Measurements	dimensions	Physical Characteristics-Dimensions Description	Dimension/Extent-Quantity-Unit
Measurements-Dimensions-Type			Physical Characteristics-Height	
Measurements-Dimensions-Value			Physical Characteristics-Width	
			Physical Characteristics-Depth	
Measurements-Dimensions-Unit			Physical Characteristics-Unit of Measurement	
Measurements-Scale			Physical Characteristics-Scale Description	
			Physical Characteristics-Scale	
MATERIALS AND TECHNIQUES				
Materials and Techniques-Description	Materials and Techniques		Physical Characteristics-Technique, Medium, and Support Description	
Materials and Techniques-Processes or Techniques		processTechnique		Creation Technique/Method/Process

VRA Core Categories	REACH	USMARC	Dublin Core
W1. Work Type	Field #1: Type of Object	655 Genre-Form	Type [or, Source.Type]
		300a Physical Description-Extent	
			Subject [or, Source.Subject]
			Description [or, Source.Description]
W2. Title	Field #4: Object Name/Title	24Xa Title and Title-Related Information	Title [or, Source.Title]
		562c Copy and Version Identification Note-Version Identification	Description [or, Source.Description]
		250 Edition Statement	
W3. Measurements	Field #7: Dimensions	340b Physical Medium-Dimensions	
		300c Physical Description-Dimensions	
W5. Technique	Field #5: Techniques/Processes	340d Physical Medium-Information Recording Technique	

CDWA	Object ID	CIMI Schema	FDA	MESL
Materials and Techniques-Processes or Techniques-Name			Physical Characteristics-Technique	
Materials and Techniques-Processes or Techniques-Implement			Physical Characteristics-Technique	
Materials and Techniques-Materials [Materials and Techniques-Materials-Role		materialMedium	Physical Characteristics-Medium	Materials/Medium
and Materials and Techniques-Materials-Name]			Physical Characteristics-Support	Support
FACTURE				
PHYSICAL DESCRIPTION	Distinguishing Features	physicalDescription		
INSCRIPTIONS/MARKS	Inscriptions and Markings	inscriptionMark	Physical Characteristics-Inscription Description	Marks/Inscriptions
			Physical Characteristics-Inscription	
CONDITION/EXAMINATION HISTORY	Distinguishing Features	condition		
CONSERVATION/TREATMENT HISTORY	Distinguishing Features			
CREATION (core)				
Creation-Creator (core)	Maker	creatorGeneral	Origin/Maker-Responsibility Description (core)	
			Related People/Corporate Bodies-Description	
Creation-Creator-Identity-Names (core)		creatorName	Origin/Maker-Name (core)	Creator/Maker-Name (required)
			Related People/Corporate Bodies-Name	
Creation-Creator-Identity-Dates				
Creation-Creator-Identity-Dates/Location-Birth (core)		creatorDateofBirth		
Creation-Creator-Identity-Dates/Location-Death (core)		creatorDateofDeath		
Creation-Creator-Identity-Nationality/Culture/Race (core)		creatorNationality-CultureRace		Creator/Maker-Culture/Nationality
Creation-Creator-Role (core)		creatorRole	Origin/Maker-Role (Broad) (core)	Creator/Maker-Role
			Origin/Maker-Role (Narrow) (core)	
			Related People/Corporate Bodies-Related Role	
Creation-Date (core)	Date or Period	dateofOrigin	Date of Execution-Descriptive Date (core)	Creation Begin Date
			Date of Execution-Earliest Date (core)	Creation End Date
			Date of Execution-Latest Date (core)	

VRA Core Categories	REACH	USMARC	Dublin Core
W4. Material	Field #6: Medium/Materials	340a Physical Medium-Material Base and Configuration	
			Format [or, Source.Format]
		562a Copy and Version Identification- Identifying Markings	
		583l Action Note-Status	
		583x or 583z Action Notes- Nonpublic or Public Note	
W6.Creator	Field #10: Creator/Maker	1XX Main Entry 7XX Added Entry	Creator [or, Source.Creator]
	Field #11: Dates of Creator/Maker	1XXd Main Entry- Associated Dates 7XXd Added Entry- Associated Dates	
W15.Nationality/Culture	Field #12: Nationality/Culture of Creator/Maker	65X Subject Index Term 545a Biographical or Historical Data	
W7.Role		1XXe Main Entry- Relator Term 7XXe Added Entry- Relator Term	
W8.Date	Field #2: Date of Creation/Date Range	260c Imprint- Date of Publication	Date [or, Source.Date]

CDWA	Object ID	CIMI Schema	FDA	MESL
Creation-Place		placeofOrigin		Creation Place
Creation-Commission-Commissioner		association-name	Related People/Corporate Bodies-Name	
OWNERSHIP/COLLECTING HISTORY				
Ownership/Collecting History-Description		owner provenance	Provenance-Provenance Description	
Ownership/Collecting History-Owner		owner provenance	Provenance-Former Owner Name	
Ownership/Collecting History-Transfer Mode				Accession Method
Ownership/Collecting History-Credit Line		creditLine		Credit Line (required)
COPYRIGHT/RESTRICTIONS		copyrightRestriction	Internal Documentation-Restrictions	
STYLES/PERIODS/GROUPS/MOVEMENTS		stylePeriod		Concepts/Style-Period
		periodName		
SUBJECT MATTER (core)				
Subject Matter-Description	Subject	contentGeneral	Method of Representation/Point of View-Method/View Description	Concept/Subject
Subject Matter-Description-Indexing Terms (core)		subject	Method of Representation/Point of View-Method/View (Broad)	
			Method of Representation/Point of View-Method/View (Narrow)	
Subject Matter-Identification-Indexing Terms (core)		subject	Subject/Built Work Identification-Subject/Built Work Name (core)	
CONTEXT		associationGeneral		Associated Events, People, Organizations, Places
Context-Architectural				
Context-Historical/Cultural		contextHistorical		
Context-Archaeological		contextArchaeological		
EXHIBITION/LOAN HISTORY			Exhibition History	

VRA Core Categories	REACH	USMARC	Dublin Core
	Field #3: Place of Origin/Discovery (also possibly CDWA Context-Archeological)	651 Subject Term-Geographical Name 752 Hierarchical Place Name	
		7XX Added Entry 536 Funding Information Note	
		561a Ownership and Custodial History-History	
	Field #13: Current Owner Field #17: Provenance	6XX Subject Access Fields	
		541c Immediate Source of Acquisition-Method of Acquisition	
		541ac Immediate Source of Acquisition and Method of Acquisition	
		540a Terms Governing Use and Reproduction	Rights [or, Source.Rights]
W14.Style/Period/ Group/Movement	Field #9: Style/Period/Group/ Movement/School	65X Subject Index Term	Description [or, Source.Description]
	Field #8: Subject Matter	520 Summary, etc.	Description [or, Source.Description]
W16. Subject		65X Subject Index Term	Subject [or, Source.Subject]
W16. Subject		65X Subject Index Term	Subject [or, Source.Subject]
W13. Original Site W14. Current Site		651 Subject Access-Geographic Name 752 Hierarchical Place Name	Coverage [or, Source.Coverage] or Subject [or, Source.Subject]
	Field #3: Place of Origin/Discovery		
W13.Original Site W14. Current Site	Field #3: Place of Origin/Discovery	651 Subject Access-Geographic Name 752 Hierarchical Place Name	Coverage [or, Source.Coverage] or Subject [or, Source.Subject]
		585a Exhibitions Note	

CDWA	Object ID	CIMI Schema	FDA	MESL
RELATED WORKS		relatedObjects relatedObjects-rendition	Related Groups/Items	
Related Works-Relationship Type				
Related Works-Identification				
RELATED VISUAL DOCUMENTATION		mrObject		
Related Visual Documentation- Relationship Type		mrObject-resourceType		
Related Visual Documentation- Image Type				
Related Visual Documentation- Image Measurements		mrObject- Description		
Related Visual Documentation- Image Ownership-Owner's Name		mrObject- publisher		
Related Visual Documentation- Image Ownership-Owner's Numbers				
Related Visual Documentation- View		mrObject- coverage		
Related Visual Documentation- View-Indexing Terms		mrObject- subjectKeyword		
Related Visual Documentation- Image Source-Name				
Related Visual Documentation- Image Source-Number		Rendition- resourceIdentifier renditionIdentifier		Accompanying Image- File Name
Related Visual Documentation- Remarks				Accompanying Image- Caption (required)
				Accompanying Image- Capture Data
RELATED TEXTUAL REFERENCES		relatedTextualReferences	Bibliographic References- Short Citation	
			Bibliographic References- Page Reference	
Related Textual References- Identification				Accompanying Document-File Name
Related Textual References-Type				Accompanying Document-Type
Related Textual References-Work Illustrated			Bibliographic References- Published Reproductions	
CRITICAL RESPONSES				
CATALOGING HISTORY			Internal Documentation- Note	
Cataloging History-Language				

VRA Core Categories	REACH	USMARC	Dublin Core
	Field #20: Related Objects	580 Linking Entry Complexity Note 787 Nonspecific Relationship Entry	Relation
W18. Relationship Type		787g Nonspecific Relationship Entry- Relationship Information	
W17. Related Works		787n Nonspecific Relationship Entry-Note	
	Field #19: Electronic Location & Access		
		533a Reproduction Note- Type of Reproduction	Relation
V1. Visual Document Type		533e Reproduction Note- Physical Description	
V3. Visual Document Measurements		533e Reproduction Note- Physical Description	
V5. Visual Document Owner		533c Reproduction Note- Agency Responsible for Reproduction	
V6. Visual Document Owner Number		533n Reproduction Note- Note about Reproduction	
V7. Visual Document View Description		245p Title-Name of Part or Section of Work 505 Contents 520 Summary, etc.	
V8. Visual Document Subject		65X Subject Index Term	
V9. Visual Document Source		533n Reproduction Note- Note about Reproduction	
		035 System Control Number	
		581 Publications about Described Materials	Relation
		581 Publications about Described Materials	
		510 Citation/Reference Note	
	Field #18: Language		

CDWA	Object ID	CIMI Schema	FDA	MESL
Cataloging History-Remarks			Internal Documentation-Sources	
CURRENT LOCATION (core)				
Current Location-Repository Name (core)		repositoryName	Group/Item Identification-Repository Name (core)	Holding Institution (required)
			Group/Item Identification-Administrative Unit (core)	
Current Location-Geographic Location (core)		repositoryPlace	Group/Item Identification-Repository Geographic Location (core)	
Current Location-Repository Numbers (core)			Group/Item Identification-Group/Item ID (core)	Accession Number (required)
			Group/Item Identification-Alternate ID	
DESCRIPTIVE NOTE	Description		Descriptive Note (core)	Description
			Purpose-Purpose Description	

Note on Mapping:

Elements are matched at the highest level of correspondence and are understood to encompass all relevant subelements of corresponding data sets. Alternative Dublin Core elements are specified in square brackets for cases in which the source element is used to describe an original from which a visual document of some sort has been derived. Elements that are not in square brackets are understood to pertain to a description of the original object rather than a reproduction, which is indicated through the relation element.

Finally, since the element sets above were developed to meet different needs and for different communities, the conceptual and semantic models that give them coherence are often subtly different even when the elements correspond. Consequently, the equivalence may inevitably seem forced in some cases. This mapping is preliminary in nature and details may change in future iterations as feedback is received from members of each of the communities represented by the data element sets included in the mapping.

VRA Core Categories	REACH	USMARC	Dublin Core
W9.Repository Name	Field #14: Current Repository Name	535a Location of Originals/Duplicates-Custodian	
W10.Repository Place	Field #15: Current Repository Place	535bc Location of Originals-Address and Country	
W11.Repository Number	Field #16: Current Object I.D. Number	035 System Control Number	
W19.Notes	Field #21: Notes	5XX General Notes	

Conclusion

This publication is owed to the efforts of several people in different places (Southern California, Northern California, Great Britain) with shared interests and different perspectives, working together toward a common goal. Although each contributor brought his or her own viewpoint and insights to the complex topic of metadata, it is gratifying to note that many commonalities run through the book: Each author stresses the urgent need for standards based on consensus from the interested communities; each states that only with consistently used, carefully crafted metadata standards will the chaotic mass of information available worldwide on networks truly become a digital library. Two of the authors, unbeknownst to one another, used the metaphor of the Rosetta Stone, the ancient Egyptian stone that provided the key to deciphering hieroglyphic writing. Indeed, the intelligent use of carefully thought-out metadata standards can provide a map to navigating the huge amount of information now available in digital form.

Another common thread that runs throughout this publication is that of collaboration: In the Information Age, we can no longer afford to be loners, working in isolation with no idea what others are doing. We must work together to pave the way to new paths to knowledge.

Glossary

administrative metadata

Metadata used in managing and administering information resources, e.g., location or donor information.

algorithm

A formula for solving a problem. An algorithm is a set of steps in a very specific order, such as a mathematical formula or the instructions in a computer program. Computer processes are governed by algorithms.

attribute

A named property of a data element, such as "level of description"; permitted values for an attribute might include "collection," "file," or "item."

back-end database

A database that provides data for an information system, distinct from the presentation or interface components of that system.

CGI script

A computer program, most frequently written in C, Perl, or a shell script, that uses the Common Gateway Interface (CGI) standard and provides an interactive interface between a user or an external computer application and a World Wide Web server. GCI script is most commonly used to develop forms that allow users to submit information to a Web server.

content model

A model that defines metadata and data structures, including the types of elements and subelements they contain.

data content standard

The rules or guidelines that govern the order, syntax, and form in which data values are entered into a data structure, e.g., *Anglo-American Cataloguing Rules*, or *Archives, Personal Papers, and Manuscripts: A Cataloging Manual for Archival Repositories, Historical Societies, and Manuscript Libraries*.

data structure standard

A standard that defines the categories or "containers" into which information is to be divided. This type of standard specifies what constitutes a record, and defines categories of information, or data fields, and their relationships. Examples are *Categories for the Description of Works of Art*, the MARC format, and the Visual Resources Association Core Categories.

data value standard

Thesauri, authority files, lexicons, or word lists that govern which terms are entered into a data structure, e.g., *Art & Architecture Thesaurus*, *Library of Congress Subject Headings*, *ICONCLASS*, or *Union List of Artist Names*.

default values

Values supplied automatically by a computer system if a human being does not specify an alternative value.

descriptive metadata

Metadata used to describe or identify information resources, e.g., cataloging records, URNs (which see), and specialized indexes.

domain name

The address that identifies an Internet or other network site. Domain names typically consist of at least two parts: the name of the company, institution, or other organization, and the highest subdomain, e.g., www.gii.getty.edu, where getty is the company or organization and gii is the highest subdomain. In other words, a domain name is a hierarchically structured namespace that acts as an alias for a range of Internet (IP) addresses. For example, the "ac.uk" domain identifies a series of IP addresses within the UK academic Internet domain.

DTD

Document Type Definition, a formal specification of the structural elements and markup definitions to be used in encoding certain types of documents in SGML (which see). Instances of DTDs include EAD, MARC, and TEI (which see).

Dublin Core

A minimal set of metadata elements that digital document creators or cataloguers can assign to information resources, which can then be used for network resource discovery, especially on the World Wide Web.

EAD

Encoded Archival Description, an SGML DTD that represents a highly structured way to create digital finding aids for a collection of archival materials.

element

A discrete component of data or metadata. Sometimes elements also contain subcomponents or subelements, e.g., a data element "language" might have the subelements "language used in the cataloging record" and "language of the material being described by the cataloging record."

encoding analog

A mapping between a specific metadata element in an SGML DTD (which see) and an equivalent in an alternative metadata set.

encoding ("marking up") information

A way for a creator of a digital object to structure and mark up text or other data so that it can be manipulated by a computer or a user, transmitted and searched over a network, or displayed to a user in the same way as it was viewed by the creator.

file transfer protocol (FTP)

A method of moving or transferring files between computers on the Internet.

header metadata

Metadata entered by the creator of a digital information resource into the header part of a file for file description and management purposes.

hostname

An identifier for a specific machine on the Internet. The hostname identifies not only the machine, but also its subnet and domain.

HTML

HyperText Markup Language, an SGML-derived markup language used to create documents for World Wide Web applications. HTML emphasizes design rather than the representation of document structure and data elements.

HTTP

HyperText Transfer Protocol, a standard protocol that enables users with Web browsers to access HTML documents and external media.

hyperlink

An abbreviated reference to a "hypertext link." Hyperlinks, indicated by encoded tags, make it possible to determine nonlinear ways to move around and between digital documents, or to link to related objects such as image or audio files.

hypermedia

A technique that links information of diverse types, frequently in nonlinear ways. Links are embedded in text and other media through the insertion of encoded tags that are invisible to the user. Generally users are alerted to the existence of a link by underlined text. When the user points to the link and selects it, the linkage is activated and the associated information is revealed.

information object

A digital item or group of items, regardless of type or format, that a computer can address or manipulate as a single object.

Internet

A global collection of computer networks that exchange information by the TCP/IP suite of networking protocols. See http://www.fnc.gov/Internet_res.html.

Internet directory

A thematically organized list of descriptive links to Internet sites, often created by humans who have classified sites by their content.

Internet search engine (spider, crawler, robot)

A software program that collects information taken from the metadata and content of files available on the Internet and places them in a database that Internet users can search in a variety of ways. The search results then provide links back to the original location of the files matching the user's search.

ISP

Internet Service Provider, an organization that provides access to the Internet, typically on a commercial basis.

legal requirements metadata

Metadata documenting or tracking legal requirements associated with access to, or usage of, information resources, e.g., privacy and access or rights and reproduction requirements.

MARC

MAchine-Readable Cataloging, a set of standardized data structures used to describe bibliographic materials that facilitate co-operative cataloging and data exchange in bibliographic information systems.

markup language

A formal way of annotating a document or collection of digital data using specially embedded encoding tags to indicate the structure of the document or datafile and the contents of its data elements. This markup also provides a computer with information about how to process and display marked-up documents.

metadata

Literally, "data about data," metadata includes data associated with either an information system or an information object for purposes of description, administration, legal requirements, technical functionality, use and usage, and preservation.

MIME (Multi-purpose Internet Mail Extension)

A set of specifications that makes it possible to interchange text in languages with different character sets as well as multimedia e-mail among different computer systems that use Internet mail standards.

multimedia

Digital materials, documents, or products, such as World Wide Web pages, CD-ROMs, or components of digital libraries and virtual museums that use any combination of text, numeric data, still and moving images, animation, sound, and graphics.

nesting

The way in which subelements may be contained within larger elements, resulting in multiple levels of metadata.

network bandwidth

This expression is derived from the term used to describe the size or "width" of the frequencies that carry analog communications such as television and radio. For Internet purposes, bandwidth is essentially a measure of the rate of data transfer.

"on the fly"

An expression used to describe computing events that are not hard-coded into the computer but that take place on demand, e.g., the generation of a set of retrieved data customized according to the user's preferences, or the conversion upon request of SGML-encoded material to HTML for presentation to a user who lacks an SGML viewer.

preservation metadata

Metadata related to the preservation management of information resources, e.g., metadata used to document, or created as a result of, preservation processes performed on information resources.

protocol

A specification—often a standard—that describes how computers will communicate with each other.

resource discovery

The process of searching for specific information on the Internet.

search engine

A program that allows users to search an information system. A search engine may provide users with a variety of ways to search.

SGML

Standard Generalized Markup Language, an ISO (International Organization for Standardization) standard, first used by the publishing industry, for defining, specifying, and creating digital documents that can be delivered, displayed, linked, and manipulated in a system-independent manner.

spamming

(used in reference to "keyword" metatags) The abuse of metadata that creators include in the HTML header area of their Web pages in order to increase the number of visitors to a Web site. Keyword spamming entails repeating keywords multiple times in order to appear at the top of search engine result listings, or listing keywords that are irrelevant to the site in order to attract visitors under false pretenses. See http://www.the grid.net/clear/spam.htm.

tags

Short, formal mnemonics used to indicate data or metadata elements, especially in HTML and SGML markup (e.g,, <TITLE>, <META>).

TCP/IP

Transmission Control Protocol/ Internet Protocol, the ISO standardized suite of network protocols that enable institutional information systems to link to other information systems on the Internet, regardless of their computer platform. TCP and IP are two software communication standards used to allow multiple computers to talk to each other in an error-free fashion.

technical metadata

Metadata created for, or generated by, a computer system, relating to how the system or its content behaves or needs to be processed.

TEI

Text Encoding Initiative, an international cooperative effort to develop generic guidelines for a standard encoding scheme for scholarly text.

URL

Uniform Resource Locator (also referred to as Universal Resource Locator), an Internet address that tells a user how and where to locate a specific file on the World Wide Web. A URL includes not only the name of a file, but also the name of the host computer, the directory path to get to that file, and the protocol needed in order to use it (e.g., http://www.gii.getty.edu/aat_browser).

URN

Uniform Resource Name (also referred to as Universal Resource Name/Number), a unique location-independent identifier of a file available on the Internet. The file remains accessible by its URN regardless of changes that might occur in its host and directory path.

use metadata

Metadata, generally automatically created by the computer, that relates to the level and type of use of an information system.

Web host

Web "hosting" refers to the storage of a Web site or home page on a server so that it can be accessed over the World Wide Web. High-quality Web hosting services are the foundation of a successful Internet presence. The quality of a Web hosting service is defined by several considerations: the speed of the Web server's connection to the Internet, the type of hardware and software used for the server, and the types of advanced services (such as CGI scripting) offered.

WHOIS++

An evolving standard for an Internet directory services protocol.

World Wide Web

A wide-area client-server architecture for retrieving hypermedia documents over the Internet. The World Wide Web also supports a means of searching remote information sources such as bibliographies, telephone directories, and instruction manuals. See http://www.w3.org/MarkUp/HTMLPlus/html plus_3.html.

XML

Extensible Markup Language, a simplified subset of SGML that is designed specifically for use with the World Wide Web and that provides for more sophisticated data structuring and validation than does HTML.

Z39.50

An ANSI (American National Standards Insitute) standard information retrieval protocol that allows a search application to submit a query to databases regardless of the kind of hardware or software the database uses. Originally implemented in the library world, Z39.50 is now gaining international acceptance for general information retrieval.

see also:

Glossary of Networking Terms (http://www.cis.ohio-state.edu/htbin/rfc/rfc1208.html)

NetGlos—The Multilingual Glossary of Internet Terminology (http://wwli.com/translation/netglos/netglos.html)

WWW Glossary (http://www.eelab.newpaltz.edu/~hillo/www.wwwgloss.html)

Glossary compiled by Murtha Baca, Tony Gill, Anne Gilliland-Swetland, and Christina Yamanaka.

Acronyms Used in This Guide, with Selected Web Addresses

AACR2
Anglo-American Cataloguing Rules
(2nd edition)

AAH
Association of Art Historians
http://scorpio.gold.ac.uk.aah/

AAT
Art & Architecture Thesaurus
http://www.gii.getty.edu/vocabulary/aat.html

ACN
Advisory Committee on Networking
http://www.jisc.ac.uk/acn/index.html

ADAM
Art, Design, Architecture & Media Information Gateway
http://adam.ac.uk/

AGOCG
Advisory Group on Computer Graphics
http://www.agocg.ac.uk/

AHDS
Arts & Humanities Data Service
http://ahds.ac.uk/

AMICO
Art Museum Image Consortium
http://www.amn.org/AMICO/

ANR
Access to Network Resources
http://ukoln.ac.uk/elib/lists/anr.html

ARLIS
Art Libraries Society
http://caroline.eastlib.ufl.edu:80/arlis/

BHA
Bibliography of the History of Art
www.gii.getty.edu/bha/index.html

Biz/Ed
Business Education on the Internet
http://www.bizednet.bris.ac.uk:8080/

CAIN
Conflict Archive on the Internet
http://www.ulst.ac.uk/cain/index.htm

CALT
Committee on Awareness, Liaison and Training
http://www.jisc.ac.uk/calt/index.html

CDWA
Categories for the Description of Works of Art
http://www.gii.getty.edu/cdwa
CDWA cataloging examples:
http://www.ahip.getty.edu/cdwa/examples/home3.htm

CEI
Committee for Electronic Information
http://www.jisc.ac.uk/cei/index.html

CHArt
Computers and the History of Art
http://www.hart.bbk.ac.uk/chart/chart.html

CHIN
Canadian Heritage Information Network
http://www.pch.gc.ca

CIMI
Computer Interchange of Museum Information
http://www.cimi.org
The CIMI Schema:
http://www.cimi.org/downloads/ProfileFinalMar98/cimiprofile4.htm#6.4.3.2.

CTI
Computers in Teaching Initiative
http://info.ox.ac.uk/cti/

DC
Dublin Core
http://www.oclc.org:5046/research/dublin_core/

DDC
Dewey Decimal System

DHS
Design History Society
http://www.sequence.co.uk/dhs/June97

ECSTASY
Enhanced Collaboration with Shared Tools for Art and Design Systems
http://www.rave.ac.uk/ecstasy/

EEVL
Edinburgh Engineering Virtual Library
http://eevl.icbl.hw.ac.uk/

eLib
Electronic Libraries Programme
http://ukoln.ac.uk/elib/

FDA
Foundation for Documents of Architecture:
A Guide to the Description of Architectural Drawings
http://www.gii.getty.edu/fda

GII
Getty Information Institute
http://www.gii.getty.edu

GLADNet
Group for Learning in Art & Design Network
http://www.mailbase.ac.uk/lists-f-j/gladnet/

HEDS
Higher Education Digitisation Service
http://heds.herts.ac.uk/

HEFCs
Higher Education Funding Councils
http://www.niss.ac.uk/education/hefc/index.html

HTML
HyperText Markup Language

IAFA
Internet Anonymous FTP Archives
http://www.roads.lut.ac.uk/System-docs/Internet-drafts/draft-ietf-iiir-publishing-03.txt

ICOM
International Council of Museums
http://www.icom.org

IHR-Info
Institute for Historical Research Information
Gateway
http://ihr.sas.ac.uk/

ISO
International Organization for Standardization
http://www.iso.ch/

JISC
Joint Information Systems Committee
http://www.jisc.ac.uk/

MDA
Museum Documentation Association
http://www.open.gov.uk/mdocassn/index.
htm#MDAHomePage

MESL
Museum Educational Site Licensing Project
http://www.gii.getty.edu/mesl/

MODELS
Moving to a Distributed Environment for
Library Systems
http://www.ukoln.ac.uk/models/intro.html

NPO
National Preservation Office
http://www.bl.uk/services/preservation/

Object ID
http://www.gii.getty.edu/pco

OCLC
Online Computer Library Center
http://www.oclc.org/

OMNI
Organising Medical Networked Information
http://omni.ac.uk/

REACH
Record Export for Art and Cultural Heritage
http://www.rlg.org/reach.html

RLG
The Research Libraries Group
http://www.rlg.org

ROADS
Resource Organisation and Discovery System
http://ukoln.ac.uk/roads/

SCRAN
Scottish Cultural Resources Access Network
http://www.scran.ac.uk/

SOSIG
Social Science Information Gateway
http://sosig.ac.uk/

SuperJANET
Super Joint Academic Network
http://www.ja.net/

TASC
Technology Applications Sub-Committee
http://www.jisc.ac.uk/tasc/index.html

TGN
Getty Thesaurus of Geographic Names
http://www.gii.getty.edu/vocabulary/tgn.html

TLTP
Teaching and Learning Technology Programme
http://www.tltp.ac.uk/

TLTSN
Teaching and Learning Technology Support
Network
http://www.tltp.ac.uk/tltsn/

UKOLN
United Kingdom Office for Library and Information Networking
http://ukoln.bath.ac.uk/

ULAN
Union List of Artist Names
http://www.gii.getty.edu/vocabulary/ulan.html

VADS
Visual Arts Data Service
http://vads.ahds.ac.uk

VISION
Visual Resources Sharing Information
Online Network
http://www.rlg.org/pr/9711vis.html
http://www.oberlin.edu/~art/vra/vision.html

VRA
Visual Resources Association
http://www.oberlin.edu/~art/vra/vra.html
VRA Core Categories:
http://www.oberlin.edu/~art/vra/wc1.html

WHOIS++
An evolving standard for an Internet
directory services protocol
http://www.nlc-bnc.ca/documents/libraries/
cataloging/metadata/whopp2.txt

W3C
World Wide Web Consortium
http://www.w3.org/

Z39.50
A standard information retrieval protocol
http://www.ukoln.ac.uk/dlis/z3950/defin.html

ZEXI
Z39.50 Experimental Implementation
http://weeble.lut.ac.uk/zexi/

Compiled by Tony Gill, with Murtha Baca and
Christina Yamanaka.

Contributors

Willy Cromwell-Kessler (bl.kes@rlg.org) came to The Research Libraries Group (RLG) in 1997 from the Stanford University Libraries, where she held a number of positions. As Head of Cataloging and Coordinator for Cataloging Development, she was charged with planning for the integration of digital and other nontraditional information resources into the library online catalog. At RLG she currently participates in the work of a new Integrated Information Services Division as a Bibliographic Specialist, helping to develop the role of structured data in the functioning of a proposed network of RLG digital full-text, bibliographic, citation, and other databases. She has been active in the development of library and bibliographic standards, publishing articles and participating in the work of standards groups, most recently as the Chair of the Standards Committee of the Program for Cooperative Cataloging (PCC), which has developed several PCC core record standards. Ms. Cromwell-Kessler has an M.A. in English Literature and an M.L.S. from Indiana University, Bloomington.

Tony Gill (tony@adam.ac.uk) is the ADAM and VADS Programme Leader at the Surrey Institute of Art and Design, and is responsible for implementing the Art, Design, Architecture & Media (ADAM) Information Gateway and the Visual Arts Data Service (VADS), both of which seek to enable access to high-quality networked information in the visual arts. Prior to this, he was Technical Outreach Manager at the Museum Documentation Association (MDA), where he advised on the use of information technology for museums and galleries. He has degrees in Communication in Computing (Middlesex University) and Physics and Philosophy (King's College, London), and is currently a Ph.D. candidate at Kingston University's School of Information Systems. He is the author of a number of publications on the applications of information technology in the arts and humanities, including the *MDA Guide to Computers in Museums*. Mr. Gill has participated actively in four of the five Dublin Core workshops, has presented a number of papers on the subject of metadata, and wrote two of the Dublin Core draft "Request for Comment" documents (jointly with Paul Miller). He is a committee member of CHArt (Computers and the History of Art), the Joint Information Systems Committee Image Digitisation Initiative Implementation Group, and the Technical Advisory Service for Images Steering Group.

Anne J. Gilliland-Swetland (swetland@ucla.edu) is an Assistant Professor at the Department of Library and Information Science in the Graduate School of Education and Information Studies at the University of California, Los Angeles. Her areas of research and teaching include archival science, electronic records management, and digital asset management. Her current research is evaluating the use of the Dublin Core in a National Science Foundation-funded project, Digital Portfolio Archives in Elementary Science Learning; and of Encoded Archival Description (EAD) in the California Digital Library. She has an M.A. in English Language and Literature from Trinity College, University of Dublin; an M.S. and C.A.S. in Library and Information Science from the University of Illinois at Urbana–Champaign; and a Ph.D. in Information and Library Studies from the University of Michigan. Her dissertation explored the development of an expert assistant for the archival appraisal of electronic communications. Dr. Gilliland-Swetland is the author of numerous research and educational publications relating to the application of digital technologies in archival and museum environments, and is writing a book (jointly with Gregory Leazer) entitled *Content, Context and Structure in the Organization of Recorded Knowledge*, which will examine the development of information organization practices in a number of professional communities. She is a member of the EAD Working Group and the Council of the Society of American Archivists.

Murtha Baca (mbaca@getty.edu), Project Manager for Standards and Research Databases at the Getty Information Institute, holds a Ph.D. in Art History and Italian Literature from the University of California, Los Angeles. Her publications include translations from the Italian of numerous monographs and exhibition catalogs, six manuscripts of Leonardo da Vinci, *An Italian Renaissance Sextet: Six Tales in Historical Context* (Marsilio Publishers, 1994), and Pellegrino Artusi's *Science in the Kitchen and the Art of Eating Well* (Marsilio Publishers, 1997). With James M. Bower, she co-edited the *Union List of Artist Names* (G.K. Hall, 1994). Her recent articles include "From Authority File to Retrieval Tool: the Union List of Artist Names" (*Computers and the History of Art* vol. 6, no. 2, 1997) and "Making Sense of the Tower of Babel: A Demonstration Project in Multilingual Equivalency Work" (*Terminology: International Journal of Theoretical and Applied Issues in Specialized Communication*, 1997). She oversaw the production and publication of the *Categories for the Description of Works of Art* hypertext document and booklet, and co-edited, with Patricia Harpring, a special double issue of the journal *Visual Resources* (vol. XI, nos. 3–4, 1996) devoted to the *Categories*. She represents the Getty Information Institute on the International Terminology Working Group, whose collaborative projects include a recently completed multilingual lexicon of liturgical objects. Dr. Baca oversaw the publication in four languages of *Guidelines for Forming Language Equivalents: A Model Based on the Art & Architecture Thesaurus* (Getty Information Institute, 1996), and is currently managing a joint project with the Chilean Ministry of Education to provide Spanish-language equivalents for several of the hierarchies in the *Art & Architecture Thesaurus*.

41